my first barbecue book

This book is dedicated to my partner, Hazel, and her son, Harris. Without these two in my life, the idea for a kids barbecue book, no matter how tongue-in-cheek, would never have come about.

Massive thanks to my good friend Mark at AuthorPackages for his help in laying out and sorting the format. His creative genius far outweighs my concept and idea. Another massive thank you to Lorna at Ravensforge Books for all of her help and support. A more helpful and dedicated pair would be very hard to find.

Copyright © 2017 by Peter J Swann
All rights reserved. This book or any portion thereof
may not be reproduced or used in any manner whatsoever
without the express written permission of the publisher
except for the use of brief quotations in a book review.

Printed by CreateSpace

First Printing, 2017

ISBN 978-1-912325-06-1

Ravensforge Books
Glasgow
Scotland
United Kingdom

www.myfirstbbq.com

my first barbecue book

by Peter J Swann

This book belongs to...

....

The best animal is...

....

The tastiest animal is...

....

What sound does a... ...cow make?

What sound does a...

...lamb make?

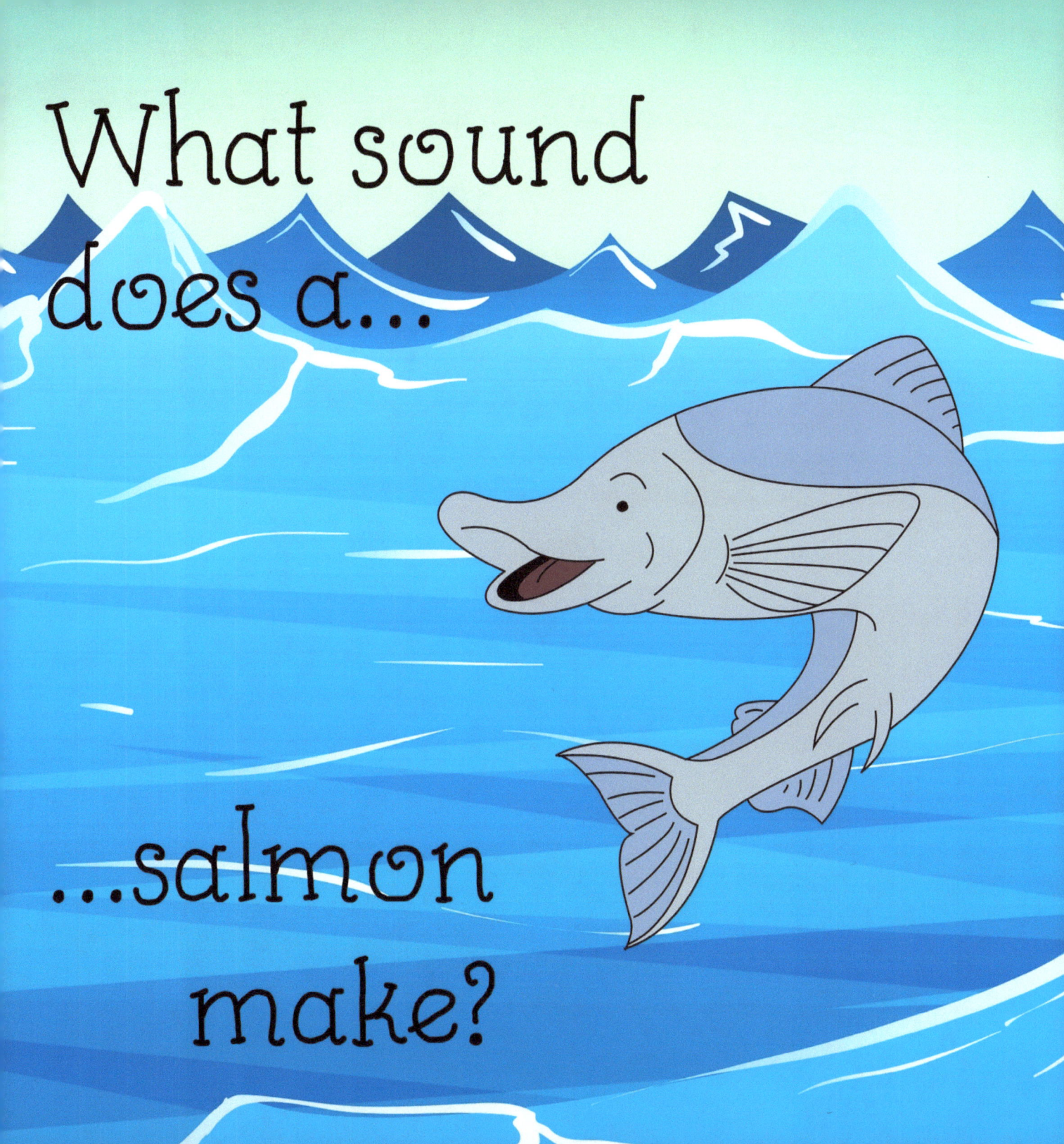

What sound does a...

...duck make?

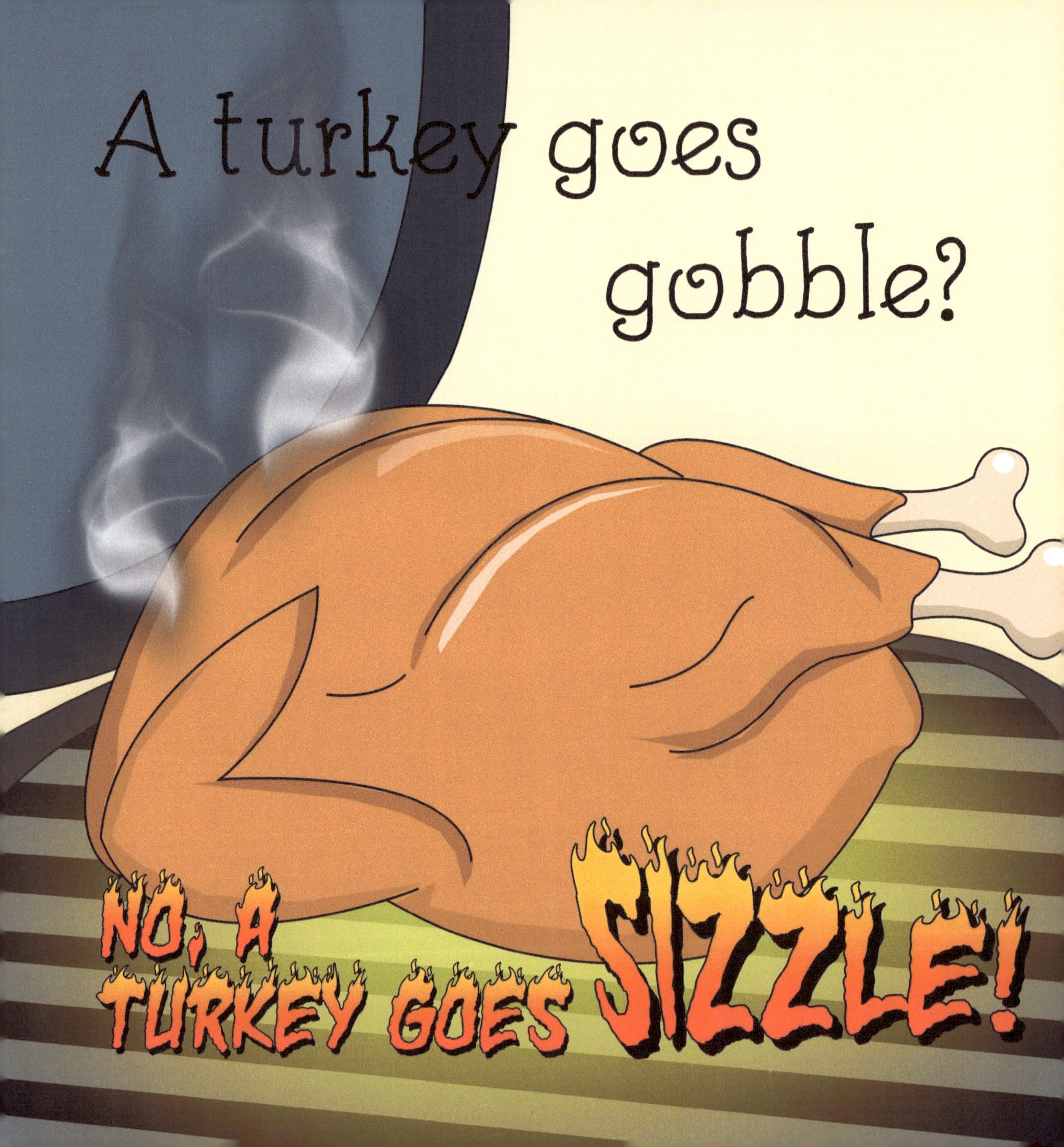
A turkey goes gobble?
NO, A TURKEY GOES SIZZLE!

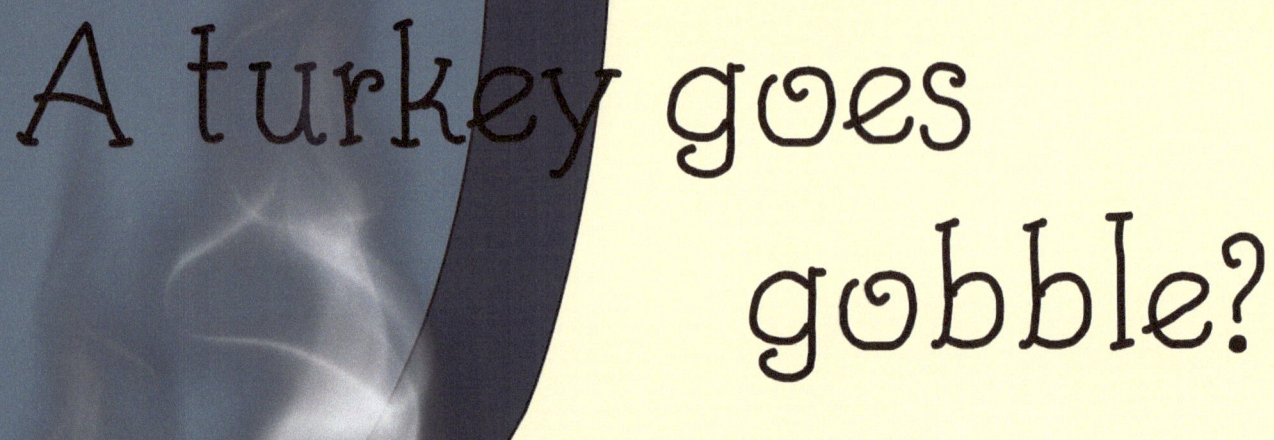

What sound does a...

...goat make?

What sound does a...

...rabbit make?

What sound does a... ...crocodile make?

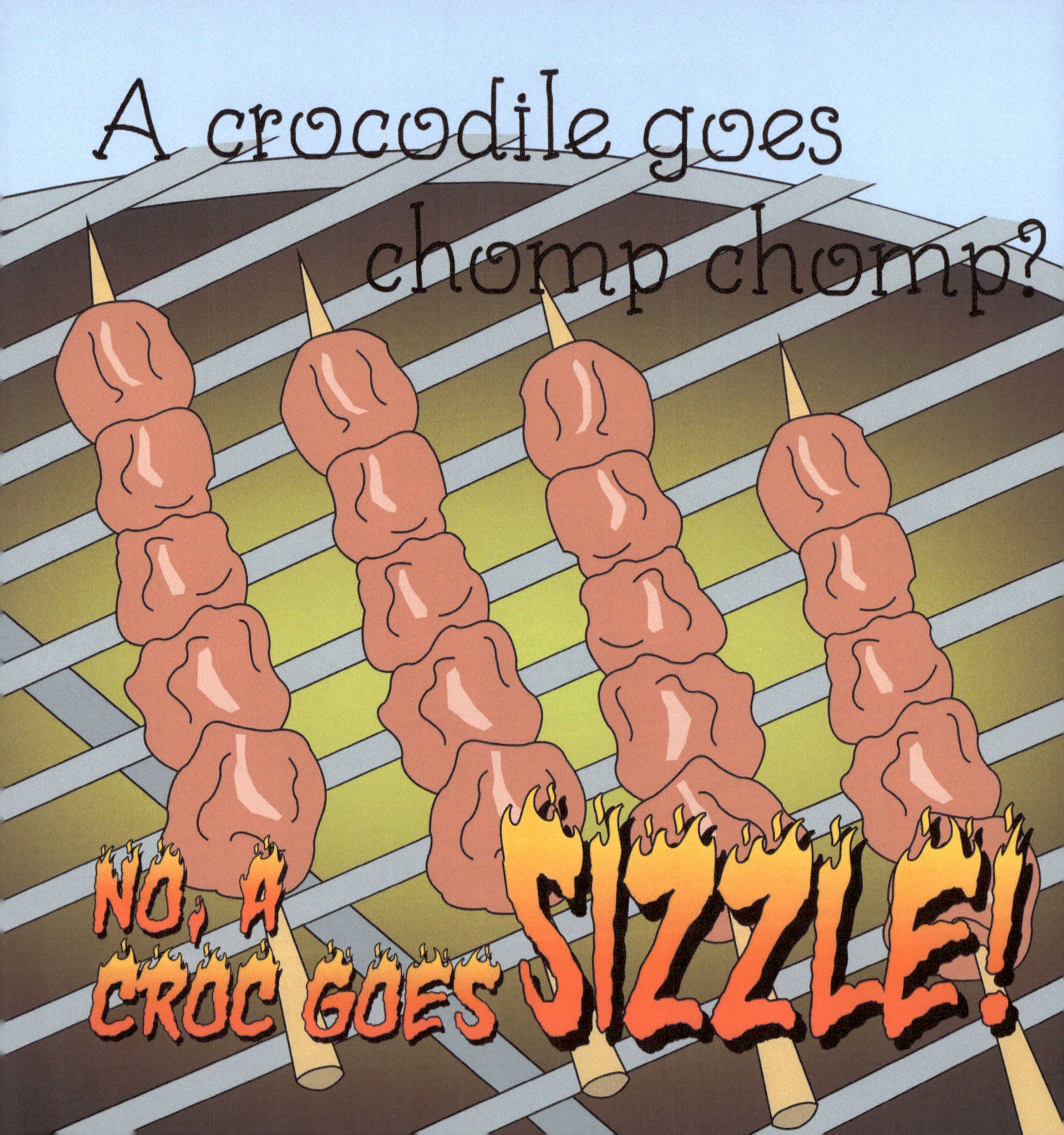

What sound does a... ...prawn make?

What sound does a... ...kangaroo make?

What sound does a... ...lobster make?

www.ingramcontent.com/pod-product-compliance
Lightning Source LLC
Chambersburg PA
CBHW041225040426
42444CB00002B/54